just enough for no one

Mulunesh Bekele

BookLeaf Publishing

Presentation by *BookLeaf Publishing*

Web: www.bookleafpub.com

E-mail: info@bookleafpub.com

ISBN: 9789357210188

First edition 2022

DEDICATION

this book is dedicated to all the women who are unfailing in their attempt to find compassion for themselves and have overcome unjust obstacles in this world and in their lives. you all have survived and for that i am inspired and thankful.

ACKNOWLEDGEMENT

it would be my pleasure to acknowledge the sisterhood of intelligent, beautiful, willing, and uplifting women who have been a part of my life and my journey on this precious earth.

complacency > abandonment

i don't want to get better
it would mean i would have to leave the little
girl i've always mourned
i've sat with her for so many years
people say the best way to care for someone in
pain is to sit with them in it
so i have
to get better would mean i would have to tell her
we must stand up and leave the place we've for
years rested
i've been an orphan for as long as i can
remember
unable to recognize my mother and father
strangers
unable to recognize the couple who took me
strangers
i don't want to get better
it would mean i would have to leave the little
girl i've always mourned
she cannot lose only person she has left

fragile

i wish i was fragile
i wish i was one of those girls that are dainty
they look effortlessly pretty just by existing
i'm jealous of their prominent collar bones
shoulders poking through their shirts and hands
that wisp around

i wish i was fragile
i wish i was one of those girls that are soft
smooth, fair, without blemish
perfect nose, full lips, fluttering eyelashes
i'm jealous of the way they make strangers stare
and captivate without even knowing

i wish i was fragile
i wish i was one of those girls that are small
their frames too little for all their pain
bodies so thin the suffering they endure feels
wrong because it's simply too exorbitant for
anyone that gentle to bear

i wish i fragile
i've been told i'm strong
more times than i'd like to hear
more than i'd like to be

my thighs are full and my arms are too large for
my liking
they swell when pushed or held

i wish i fragile
for once i want to be delicate
to be seen as breakable
to be handled with care
to be told my suffering was disproportionate to
my frame

i wish i was fragile
my body as light as the skin
i would like to have
they tell me melanin is worth more than gold
yet it's the source of my hate
my lack of value
at least the world can be cruel
but not as cruel as the girl in my skin

unavailable

hi you've reached mulunesh
leave a message
i don't answer many calls
guilty for the all the voicemails
with that blue dot on the left
i'm busy weeping over my existence
leaving my body to leave the room
thoughts entangled and caught
in the dreaded web upstairs
thinking of all the words
i should of said
the words i should've tucked into my cheek
like the pills i don't like to take
slipping down
or is it up
reality is too distorted to have direction
i apologize for my inability to tap
the green icon and speak
so please don't hate me when you hear
hi it's mulunesh leave a message

let the dead rest

i have written countess eulogies with my tears
before we even parted
and now you only exist when i speak your name
or think of you
things i no longer do
you held the key to my soul
i've since changed the locks
it is comforting to know my revenge is
you'll never look at the moon without
remembering eyes
or hear yellow lights without
remembering my voice
that you have 3000 pictures of me
i know you won't delete
i avenge myself by painting
over my illusions of you
it's comforting to know that my revenge is
unmemorizing the shape of your face
the curves of your smile
leaving our memories to sit
only letting them exist
at the time they were made
realizing i never really did meet you
in your truest form
i learned 7 years is too short

to learn who one truly is
my heart couldn't catch up to my mind
a few years too late
and now i know
you can't fight fate

home is where my sanity lies

i live nowhere
a vagrant
i live in my mind
but it is not my home
home is safe, sane
i have neither
i don't think i will find one
sometimes i make it someone else
most times my bed
occasionally a fixation
but never maintaining permanent residence
i don't mind the dysfunction
it's all i know
i don't mind the wandering
it's all i've done
i stopping searching for my sanity long ago
it's overpriced, unrealistic, unattainable

fairy tales

the only place love can survive is in the books
it lives on the shelves waiting to be opened
i found solace in other worlds
in any way to escape mine
the only place love can survive is in the books
to mock the lack of these stories in our reality

suffocated

that tightness in your throat
the one you feel in an argument
during goodbyes
when you pushed against the wall of sadness in
tears
those are the words you wanted to say but never
escaped your mouth

lost years

there's an infinite number of ways to live a good life.

there's an infinite number of choices to make
because there's an infinite number of ways to spend a night
i will never be this young again and i've lost too many years
i learned to become forgiving
of others ugliness
before i became beautiful
but being the false form of beautiful
in this world turned me to stone
because i knew a glowing soul
has no place in a world lit by man made light
i'll never be this beautiful again and i've lost too many years

we hate her

the voices in my head are back
we hate this body

i can feel the fat above her knees
i can feel the fat under her chin
i can feel the fat behind her arms
how can she live with all this skin
she sags
she folds
she keeps getting bigger

the voices in my head are back
they tell me to eat like the animal I am
eat eat eat
until it hurts
eat eat eat
then they change their mind
they tell me to never eat again
until i can't breathe
i can't breathe

the voices in my head are back
they tell me I deserve to die
die die die
it's been a year too long

kill kill kill
you can do it
they all wish you would do it

the voices in my head are back
they tell me to peel myself apart
scratch scratch scratch
the lines burn
rip rip rip
i love seeing the marks
finally a reflection of the chaos in my mind

the voices in my head are back
why won't she drown
gasp I'm gasping
where is the air
the tears won't stop
gasp I'm gasping
please help me
i can't breathe

the voices in my head are back
they tell me to do bad things to feel better
there's only one voice that wants to get better
I thought I was better

anxiety

i often die three times from misfortune
once before it the wave of pain crashes over me
and i anticipate its arrival
again when it happens,
and lastly in retrospect
if only i knew how to live in my immediate
reality
i would have many fewer deaths

treading water

i forget to drink water
so i make a cup of tea
but it my tears always run me dry again

i've tried working on rewiring my coping habits
reading self help books to unfuck my brain

but a ted talk and a notebook don't help you
tread water

i hold a universe in my rib cage
the weight of galaxies are mine to carry

and i can't hate myself for hurting still
because how many humans are left to cry for a
dying world

i cry for myself for wanting to join them all
ashamed of where i've been and what i've done
the places i've been sent to to teach me survive
my own seas

but it's hard to save anyone when you're
treading water

the cost of vulnerability

i used to write you letters
pieces of my soul in ink and paper

puzzles on the dining room table like we're 70
paper lanterns in the park
looking for the stars
now when i see cars that look like yours
my heart feels heavy
because you don't want me
at least you're too far
to find when i relapse

people say maybe in another life but i think my
soul will always remember how you broke mine

love is a mortal wound
you dug the knife in so slowly i hardly noticed
the pain until i couldn't breathe

and you left me to bleed out alone
no wonder my hands have always been so cold

i used to tell you that i loved you out of
certainty, now i say it to convince you of yours

not even the moon

on my lowest nights
not even the moon bothered to show up
my greatest confidant

not even the empress of the darkest corners of
the universe wanted to outstretch a beam of light
to my aching soul

the sea was my only company
the waves mocked the turbulence of my thoughts
the water mimicked the black depths of my heart
the mist of the ocean spray laughed at my salty
tears

and on my lowest nights
not even the moon bothered to show up

she did exactly what every being i loved and
thought loved me in return had done
she fell in line with my traitors and heart
breakers

not even the moon bothered to show up
she echoed the whispers that rose and crashed in
my mind

i don't want you anymore
you're too much for me

how foolish of me to assume permanence in
such a temporary existence

nothing can stay
nothing will stay
how could you think that i would too

when will you learn that the only consistent
piece of life is this:
you are the sole thing will be with you until the
end,
you are the one thing you could possibly count
on

ilym

you were the first person to truly love me
to learn to know me
to pay attention
to put me first

and that same person broke every promise they
ever made
every promise sealed with our pinky fingers

you were the first person to truly surprise me
how fast you left
how fast you took back your love
how easy it was to drive away
how easy it was to never see me again
how easy it was to never speak to me again

and i'll never know where i went wrong
what i did to make the one person who loved me
back leave me
really truly leave
was it when i started to beg to be loved
was it when i stood up for myself
was it when i realized you were flawed
was it when you met her

were you not the one
who taught me to fight back
were you not the one
who told me how much i deserve
were you not the one
who said you'd do anything for me
were you not the one
who promised me forever
to be my safe haven

at least i know now who loved who more
and you always swore it was you
and i always believed it
i hope your own love ruined you
like it ruined me

broken wings

my sanity was malnourished
because i served all my being
to the broken winged
i wrapped fallen angels
in the silk blanket of my words
i carried all the demons
that had stored within them
it's always been my job to rescue
a calling to save
a passion to heal
a task that dims your own divine
if you can't ration your time
i think that one of the best lessons they've
taught me was
it's cost my holiness, then my life
angel who's wings grew dark
that sometimes you have to let some things die

the empress has no clothes

unzipped the costume i fabricated
and stepped outside the body suit
abandoned my armor
undressed my uniform
i stared at the patched holes
and punctured parts
sat down on my knees
to redress me
scrubbing off the imprints
of hands i failed to pull of me
reclaiming the body i finally own
the freedom to customize
the chance to accessorize
septum piercing
i wear my rings
like i will learn to wear my truth
tattooed words of my mother tongue
ink stained on my skin
like i will learn to stain
permanent self-love
dressed for comfort
like the comfort i will find in
retreating to the safety of my vessel
robed with divine power
i now rule my dominion

now no one can no longer say
the empress has no clothes

spirit of discernment

the privilege of dissatisfaction
an out to the expectation of extended content
the elimination from the exhaustion of endless searching
the end of seeking eternal satisfaction
it's easier to be disappointed than enthusiastic
i don't encourage the envisionment eventual euphoria
i'm selective about my desires

pyrite

i wasn't prepared for the unconditional support
that comes from unconditional love
our harmonies aligned
but when we reached the bridge
you changed your tone
i was left singing a tune alone
while you altered the lyrics
and even with our unmatched frequencies
we couldn't find dissonance
a classic novel
the pages ripped out
the words failing to make a sentence
just like the times i tried
to rebind or hide
alchemist
lead to gold
you were fools stone
i lost my mind trying to make sense of yours
i turned my bruised hands into palms
tipped with diamonds
a resting place for a heart
i can't hold occupying
mine you sold

inferior

i think i liked you the way i liked oversized
sweatshirts
you standing a foot taller
i like things that make me feel smaller
the vastness of the universe
open fields uninhabited
cities in which i am insignificant

i like things that make me feel smaller
rooms that don't invite me
to hold space
crowds that i know i can't compete in
how easy it is to be irrelevant

gabriella

when love came knocking at my door
i opened it to see you standing
you saw me with your heart
and then your eyes
we lied on the floor
souls meeting instantly
souls joining hands
at our experiences
at our trauma
at our roles
at our values
both our brown eyes
staring back at the reflection of each other
yet seeing ourselves
you are what i am not
what i cannot be
who i hope to be
i would give you everything
to see you smile
to hear your voice
to watch you smile
i've treasured our memories
forever locked in the safe of my heart
where i keep the time capsule
of why i'd like to stay alive

to honor the privilege of knowing you
to protect the loyalty of being yours
your existence is precious to me
soul mate
soul sister

time is not a possession +
truth will never hide

i learned that it wasn't about our frame of time
but rather the frame of mind
the window frame from which looked out
the windows of my mind
the windows of our finite time
i will not shut out what i am shown
because i didn't not like the view
i will not ignore what is to be true
because i can't control what i thought i knew

www.ingramcontent.com/pod-product-compliance
Lightning Source LLC
Chambersburg PA
CBHW051753130826
49812CB00033B/1133
9789357210188